The MFIT Magazine:

(What your school will *never* teach you)

Melanin Mweusi Magik

https://mfit.productions

No 1 November 2020

Olmec stone head licensed under CC BY-SA

Stone head found on the Thames foreshore at Battersea

Dr Marie Charles & Professor Bill Boyle

1

https://www.facebook.com/museumoflondon/photos Mweusi in Swahili means black (Azikiwe, 2019, p.130)   Dedicated to the scholars who have restored, reclaimed & rescued our history.

The MFIT Magazine/number 1

November 2020

The cover of our first issue illustrates a cultural continuity which sadly is not being taught in the majority of the schools and universities of our education system. The two stone melanated heads are from two discrete locations but represent the same First Nation People. The first head is an Olmec [old Mexico] while the second was discovered at Battersea, London, on the banks of the River Thames. Read on for further detail.   Table of contents:

Preface

Welcome to the Many Faces In Teaching [MFIT] Magazine. This new resource is a publication dedicated to offer access to the histories, sciences, and civilizations of First Nation People (FNP), Moors, Melanated Global Majority (MGM), and Black. Although Black, Negro, or Persons of Colour are not nationalities and do not exist in international law and are considered "Civiliter Mortuus" or "dead" in the eyes of the law. A person of colour means *"an appearance, semblance (or symbol) or simulacrum, distinguished from that which is real. A prima facie or apparent right. Hence, a deceptive appearance; a plausible assumed exterior, concealing a lack of reality"* (Black's Law Dictionary, 4th ed). MFIT's objective is to present the real and tangible bio-chemical scientific origin of Blackness as it relates to FNP and Moors who are the descendants of the ancient Moabites, Canaanites, Phoenicians, Amorites, Firbolgs, Tuatha De Danann, Milesians, Giodels, Formarians, Nemedians, and the Parthalonians. These ancient people under many appellations, are the (so called) blacks about whom the current schooling system will never teach as truth or correct history.

This issue #1, sets out the foundation of Blackness and its basis in melanin from a scientific study. The stone heads [front cover] place the evidence within a correct geo-political and spatial orientation of our nation and other nations from the beginning.

"When you really know who you are you wouldn't want to be anybody else"
Professor Kaba Hiawatha Kamene.

https://mfit.productions

*Mor*ula

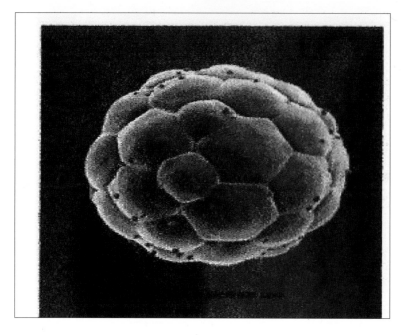

BlackBerry is the Black name of a fertilized egg and its name is *Mor*ula, a solid ball of cells resulting from a division of a fertilized ovum and from which a blastula is formed. If you are a human being, you start from a blackberry showing the ancestry of life. Two hormones are created when the *Mor*ula attaches itself to the woman's uterus called ACG- Melanocyte Stimulating Hormone which is the essence that controls black pigment cells. So, from day one Blackness is building the scaffolding of the human body. It is directing and telling DNA what to do. Melanin dictates to DNA-melanin precedes DNA (Dr Richard King, 1993).

Kemetic term	Transliteration	Translation
	km.t	(Black-land (Egypt)) [235]
	km-wr	(Big-black-one (10th nome of Lower Egypt)) aka (Big-black (region of the Bitter Lakes))
	km-wr	(great black one (Osiris))
	km	(black)
	km.y	(black one (Osiris, Min))
	km.tj	(Egyptians)

Above is a list of terms which are found in the Thesaurus Linguae Aegyptiae (TLA), an online database of the Kemetic language at the Berlin-Brandenburg Academy of Sciences and Humanities in Berlin, Germany. The terms confirm the meaning of KMT (Azikiwe, 2019, p.191)

lecture by Dr Richard King: *'Afrikan Origins of Psychiatry, December 1993.*

Africans called it _KM_ and the Greeks called it melanin the ancient Kemites represented _KM_-blackness, as a piece of wood burned at the end. This does not simply mean 'burned from a tree' as a piece all burned up, no it means infused of wood from the tree with _spirit_. This is life. This is blackness, life with deep symbolism and it being so intense that it turns black". Dr Richard King (1993) lecture.

"Black was the colour of the night sky, primeval ocean, outer space, birthplace and womb of planets, stars and galaxies. Black was the colour of carbon, the key atom found in all living matter. Carbon atoms linked together to form black melanin the first chemical that could capture light and reproduce itself. The chemical key to life and the brain itself was found to be centred around black neuromelanin" (King, 1990, p.8).

The Editors of this Magazine have assumed [cover message: _What your school will never teach_] that these focussed themes are not being taught on your syllabus. Do you agree? Let the Editors know on our website Comments section: https://mfit.productions

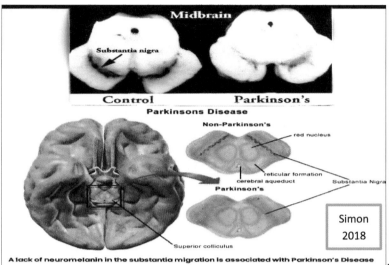

The dark pigmented neurons in the Substantia Nigra are reduced in the Parkinsonian brain. Source: Simon (2018). & Afroscientific

The Locus coeruleus (literally meaning Black Dot) is the uppermost point in an all-black neuromelanin nerve tract that runs from the brain stem into the spinal cord. Olszneki (1964) mapped the brain stem and found 12 brain sites containing pigmented (melanin) cells. These are the substantia nigra with its associated nucleus brachialis pigmentosus and nucleus paranigralis" (King, 1990, p.19). Clearly, the 'black substance' found in our bodies i.e. brain, spine etc plays a critical role in the body's capacity for healthy neurological functionality and protection against disease.

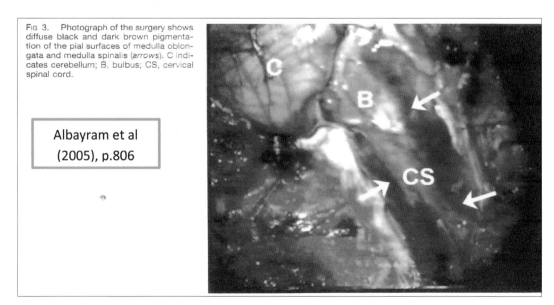

FiG 3. Photograph of the surgery shows diffuse black and dark brown pigmentation of the pial surfaces of medulla oblongata and medulla spinalis (*arrows*). C indicates cerebellum; B, bulbus; CS, cervical spinal cord.

Albayram et al (2005), p.806

Ancient knowledge of science and biology

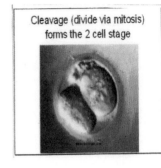

Cleavage (divide via mitosis) forms the 2 cell stage

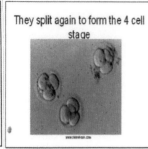

They split again to form the 4 cell stage

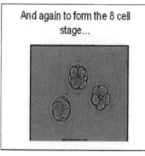

And again to form the 8 cell stage...

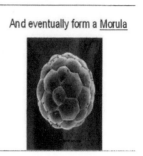

And eventually form a Morula

(https://creativecommons,org/licences/by-sa/4.0/) www.sloder.com/spitem-1015-1.html

In ancient Kemet on the coffin of Petamon are the following lines:

I am One that transforms into Two

I am Two that transforms into Four

I am Four that transforms into Eight

After this I am One.

(Coffin of Petamon, Cairo Museum no: 1160 [6]. Text from: _New light on Ancient Knowledge. Egyptian Mysteries, Lucy Lamy (1981), p.9._ **If we look at the photo showing the cell division of an embryo [above] this strongly suggests that the ancient Kemites not only understood mitosis- cell division - but revered this science in death as a cyclical process.**

https://mfit.productions

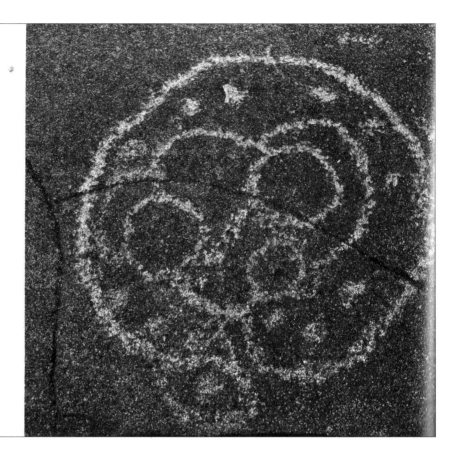

A petroglyph near Carolina, South Africa, showing a strange configuration of circles and dots that are connected by lines. The crack through the carving is an indication of the age. It is my stance that the artists would not have made the carving on a cracked rock, and especially not right over the crack. The erosion around the crack and the patina growth that has completely covered the crack are probably well over 50,000 years old, which is an indication of the age of the carving itself.

(photo used with kind permission from www.michaeltellinger.com)

This carving is from South Africa, near Carolina, and looks remarkably like the biological process mitosis or cell division as in embryo development. This rock carving has been dated to over 50,000 years old (source*: African Temples of the k. The lost Technologies of the Gold Mines of Enki by Michael Tellinger, 2013, p130.*

 In chapter One of *World's Before our Own, Brad Steiger (1978) S*teiger **argues that "There is a great deal of suppressed, ignored, and misplaced prehistorical cultural evidence that would alter the established interpretations of human origins and provide us with a much clearer definition of what it means to be human"(p.9). We argue that it is time to escape the imposed artificial and incorrect premature timeline of 6,000 years. The archaeological, anthropological, and linguistic evidence simply does not support this socially engineered paradigm.**

https://mfit.productions

Etymology of Melanin: <u>Melan</u> (root) meaning: *black, dark origin-*Greek: <u>Melas.</u> **In Robert Graves' book:** *The Greek Myths, vol 2 (1990),* **he provides a list of word derivatives related to Melanin:**

Melaenis--- black one

Melampus----black foot

Melaneus----black one

Melanion-----black native

Melanippe---- black mare

Melanippus---black stallion

Melanuis/ Melas----black

Melantheus or Melanthus---with blossoms or swarthy

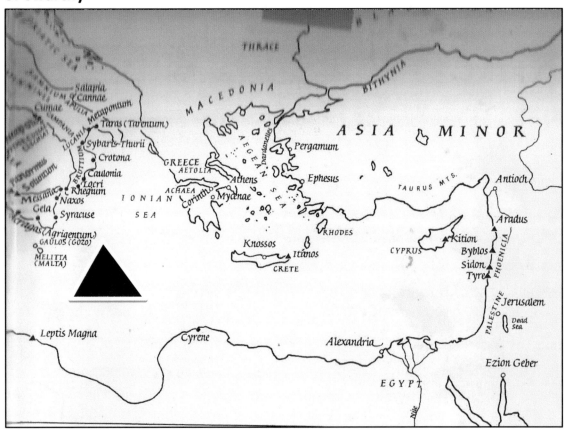

Look at the map of the Mediterranean showing the spread of Phoenician influence throughout the ancient world. Notice the original name of Malta as _Mel_itta. (*Hannibal: The struggle for Power in the Mediterranean*, De Beer, 1969, p.30).

Carbon is the basis of Melanin. Melanin is produced first in the brain which is the command centre of the body, and in the pineal gland located in the centre of the brain which is synthesised by melanocytes. Melanocytes are melanin producing neural crest-derived cells located in the bottom layer (the stratum basale) of the skin's epidermis; the middle layer of the eye (the uvea), the inner ear, vaginal epithelium (inner lining), meninges - the three membranes (dura mater, arachnoid, and pia mater) that line the skull and vertebral canal that enclose the brain and spinal cord; bones and heart. Melanin is found all over the body: "Melanin is _the_ key organising molecule in the body and it precedes DNA and tells DNA what to do...not only does melanin absorb light but has a major role in your immune system" (*Melanin: The Organising Molecule, F.E. Barr, 1983*).

"This photo is of a 35 day -old embryo and the eye is pure melanin. All of the dark/black streaks in the image are melanin. When the embryo is first formed it has a 'dark streak' all along its outline- and it is all melanin" (*Dr Karl Maret: The Science of Melanin Lecture Presentation, 2014.*)

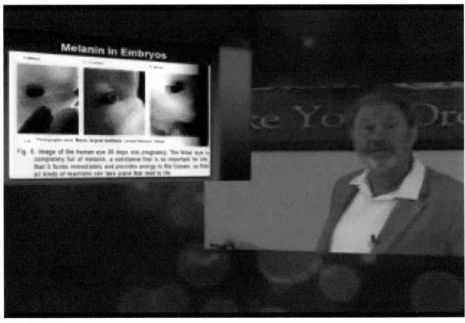

Dr Phil Valentine (2018) argues that our story has been bleached out and it is our job to put the colour back into our history. Phrases such as 'Oh, I don't see colour'; 'We should stop focusing on colour', and 'let's work towards a colour-blind approach' suggest that something more insidious is at play. Why is the schooling system not teaching the science of melanin- that is carbon and if carbon is absent there is no life? Melatonin is the hormone that is secreted from the pineal gland in the brain at night. Serotonin is secreted in the daytime opposite to melatonin, and is a neurotransmitter throughout the body which is electricity and is also responsible for your circadian rhythms i.e. when to go to sleep and when to wake up and it is our own biological alarm clock. The blackness that is building from day one of life which Dr Richard King discusses is so precious that The Oduno Scale was developed by Baba Tarik A. Oduno in which melanin is worth more than gold. How is this possible?

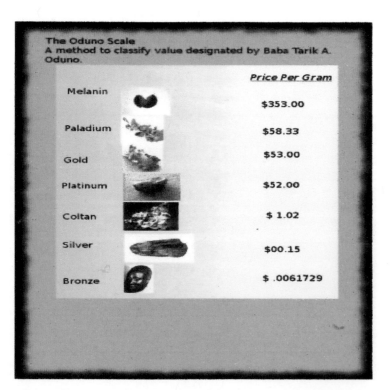

The author Nnamdi Azikiwe states that: "Melanin is a chemical and chemicals have dollar value" which he discusses in his (2019) book titled: *Melanin is Worth More than Gold. Is This The Era Of The Blessed Generation?*

The Oduno Scale is a graphic representation comparing the dollar value of melanin relative to gold, silver, platinum palladium and coltan. It is named in honor of Baba Tarik A. Oduno who inspired its creation.

The Oduno Scale (2014)

(Azikiwe, 2019, p.25)

In his book: *The African Background to Medical Science. Essays on African History, Science & Civilizations*; Dr Charles Finch describes the ancient knowledge of our ancestors through primary source artifacts such as the African Papyrus (misnomered as 'Edwin Smith Papyrus'). "A few selected cases of the 48 recorded in the Papyrus can now be considered to illustrate the scope of Egyptian medical knowledge…that this ancient physician adopts a clinical method almost identical to our own involving an examination, a diagnosis and a treatment (if indicated); all of this 35 centuries before Hippocrates. Case 8 presents a fascinating discussion of a rather rare neurological condition, the 'contre-coup' cranial injury" (p.160).

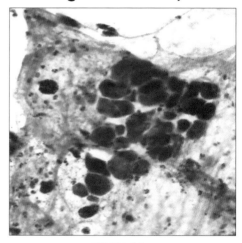

licensed under CC BY-SA

Figure 1 Extracted Melanin recording a .737 Voltage on Sunlight

Extracted Melanin

(Source: *Melanin. Energy from light and the soul's ascent* (2015). "Recently, it has been discovered by Dr Arthur Solis Herrera that melanin has the capacity to split water into diatomic hydrogen and oxygen with sunlight as a catalyst" (p.2). In addition, Del (2011) and her colleagues report in their research paper: *The Unexpected Capability of Melanin to Split the Water Molecule* : "That it was believed that only plants were capable of this, photosynthesis occurs in humans as it does in plants" (p.217).

(Photo used with kind permission from Melanin Research Foundation)

Melanin Magik

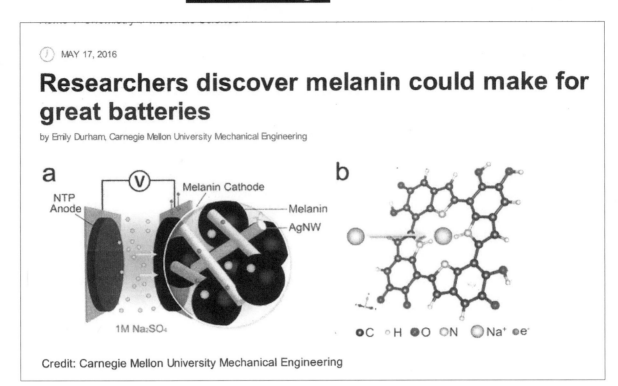

MAY 17, 2016

Researchers discover melanin could make for great batteries

by Emily Durham, Carnegie Mellon University Mechanical Engineering

Credit: Carnegie Mellon University Mechanical Engineering

A team from Carnegie Mellon University has discovered that the *chem*ical (*KM*) structure of melanin on a macromolecular scale exhibits, amongst other shapes, a four-membered ring - in other words, a chemical structure that may be conducive to creating certain kinds of batteries based on natural melanin pigments. Scientists at the City University of New York have found a way to recreate melanin's properties in a synthetic polymer. People with darker skin have lower rates of cancer, so the polymer will be used to protect the skin against sun exposure and skin damage.

(Source: www.mentalfloss.com- Ferro 2017)

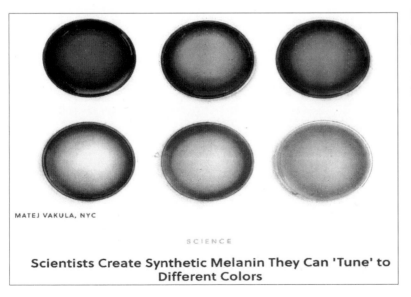

MATEJ VAKULA, NYC

SCIENCE

Scientists Create Synthetic Melanin They Can 'Tune' to Different Colors

Melanosome, Melanocyte & Melanin:

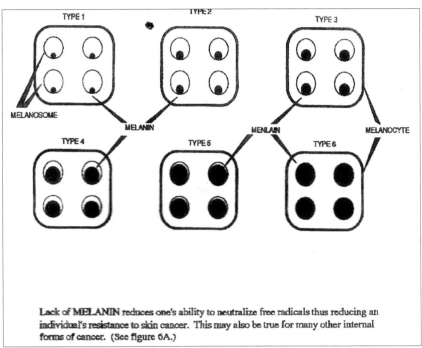

Lack of MELANIN reduces one's ability to neutralize free radicals thus reducing an individual's resistance to skin cancer. This may also be true for many other internal forms of cancer. (See figure 6A.)

Dr Carol Barnes and his book*: Melanin: The Chemical Key to Black Greatness*

Melanin or the lack of melanin may be summarised below from skin types (1-6):

TYPE 1 - These individuals are white and cannot produce MELANIN.

They have blue eyes, blond or red hair, white skin and often have freckles.

They have a Celtic background (Irish, Scottish, Welsh).

They are most prone to develop melanoma and other types of skin and organ cancer.

They show skin aging early in life between the ages of 25-30 years.

TYPE 2 - These individuals are white and produce very low levels of MELANIN.

They have hazel or blue eyes.

They have red or blond hair.

They often have freckled skin.

They are very prone to developing skin cancer.

They show skin aging early in life, between 25-30 years.

(Barnes, 2001, pp 22-23)

TYPE 3 - These individuals are white and produce moderate to low levels of MELANIN.

They have blond, brunette or lightly pigmented hair. They show a moderate to high risk of developing skin or other organ cancer.

They show skin aging by the age of 30-40 years.

TYPE 4 - These individuals are whites who are lightly tan and include Japanese, Chinese, Italian, Greeks, Spanish, and Red Indians.

They produce moderate levels of MELANIN.

They show a moderate risk of developing skin or other organ cancer.

TYPE 5 - These individuals are brown-skinned and include Mexicans, Indians, Malaysians, Puerto Ricans, and other Spanish speaking people.

They produce moderate to high levels of MELANIN.

Their eyes and hair are deep brown or black.

They show aging after the age of 50.

They seldom develop skin or other organ cancers.

TYPE 6 - These individuals are BLACK in color and include AFRICANS (EGYPTIANS, ETHIOPIANS, NIGERIANS, ETC.) AMERICAN BLACKS and AUSTRALIAN ABORIGINES!

Their eyes and hair are BLACK!

They virtually have no incidence of skin cancer!

They show skin aging after the age of 50-60 years.

SKIN TYPE	ERYTHEMA AND TANNING REACTIONS TO SUN EXPOSURE
I	ALWAYS BURN, NEVER TAN
II	USUALLY BURN, TAN LESS THAN AVERAGE (WITH DIFFICULTY)
III	SOMETIMES MILD BURN, TAN AVERAGE
IV	RARELY BURN, TAN MORE THAN AVERAGE (WITH EASE)
V	BROWN-SKINNED PERSONS
VI	BLACK-SKINNED PERSONS

Figure 10 The Fitzpatrick Scale indicating six different skin types based on the findings of Dr. Thomas B. Fitzpatrick. Four of the skin types burn after one hour of sun exposure. Two do not.

(In Azikiwe, 2019, p.27).

When we look at the descriptions of the skin types in the above charts, we must ask ourselves 'what is the psychological effect of viewing the scale as it presents hierarchically grouped skin types?' The effect of observing this information creates a reverse psychology of order in our brain when in fact, science has revealed that melanated beings are dominant and not recessive. For example, in relation to the strong desire to have a tan in leisure activities and beauty regimen Dr Francis Cress Welsing argues: "The very tanning mechanism is bombarding the cells of the skin that customarily or normally would produce melanin pigment. If those cells have a deficiency of an enzyme called tyrosinase then they cannot go forward and produce melanin pigment. But if I bombard those cells with ultraviolet rays, I can force the cells to produce small quantities of the tyrosinase enzyme and go forward to produce a melanin pigment" (in Azikiwe, 2019, p.3). Remember, Dr King reminds us on pages 4-5 that all human beings begin as a Black berry- _Mor_ula showing the ancestry to life.

Dr Francis Cress Welsing. licensed under CC BY-SA

https://mfit.productions

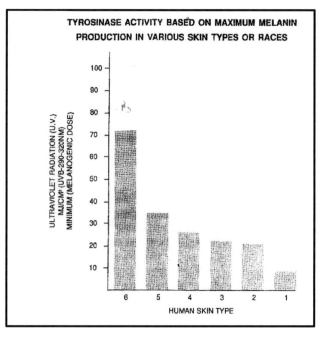

(In Barnes, 2001, p.24)

Summary

www.shutterstock.com • 1248701260

Licensed under CC by SA

Melanin is a crucial but complex subject. We wanted to raise it in this first issue of our magazine. But it will be further explained in subsequent issues. Something to think about: What would happen to the mind of a melanated child, student, or adult the next time that they heard somebody refer to them using the 'N' word? But what if they responded with the 'M' word after being grounded in the scientific and biological research presented in this magazine?

The authors are confident that their psychological faculty, at least, would be better formed to apply some of the scientific logic which the current schooling curricular fails to supply or teach. How would their learner identities emerge, grow, and develop within this pedagogical paradigm?

Our aim in this magazine is to decolonize the learning content which is offered to children/students in the education system. That aim can only be achieved if children are developed and supported to realise that they are not the passive recipients of historical facts but that they ARE history, science biology, literature, technology, and mathematics themselves.

Until next time *Ku amsha* (to awaken)

https://mfit.productions

References

Afroscientific (Nd) <u>Melanin in the brain protects it from Parkinson's disease.</u>
<u>https://www.afriscitech.com</u>

Albayram. S. Urger. E. Oz. B. Kafadar. A. Islak. C. & Kocer. N. (2005) <u>MR Imaging of Pial</u>
<u>Melanosis Secondary Posterior Fossa Melanotic Ependymoma</u>. American Journal of
Neuroradiology, 26, pp 804-808.

Azikiwe. N (2019<u>) Melanin is Worth More Than Gold. Is this the Era of the Blessed</u>
<u>Generation?</u> The Mhotep Corporation, Maryland, USA.

Barr. F.E. Saloma. J. S. & Buchele. M. J. (1983) <u>Melanin: The Organising Molecule. Medical</u>
<u>Hypotheses</u>, May 11 (1), pp 1-139.

Barnes. C (2001) <u>Melanin: The Chemical Key to Black Greatness</u>. Lushena Books, Illinois,
USA.

Del. M. Arias-Esparza. M. Isabel. R. & Arias. S. (2011) <u>The Unexpected Capability of Melanin</u>
<u>to Split the Water Molecule and the Alzheimer's Disease</u>. Neuroscience & Medicine, 2 (2),
pp. 217-221.

Durham. E. (2016) <u>Researchers discover melanin could make for great batteries</u>.
<u>https://phys.org/news/2016-05-melanin-great-batteries.html</u>

Ferro. S. (2017) <u>Scientists Create Synthetic Melanin they can 'tune' to different colors</u>
<u>https://www.mentalfloss.com</u>

Finch. C. S. (1990) <u>The African Background to Medical Science. Essays on African History,</u>
<u>Science & Civilizations.</u> Karnak House, London, UK.

Kamene. K.H. (2019) Spirituality Before Religions. Spirituality is unseen science...Science is
seen spirituality. <u>www.kabakamene.com</u>

King. R. (1990) <u>African Origin of Biological Psychiatry</u>. Lushena Books Inc, Chicago, USA.

King. R. (1993) <u>Afrikan Origins of Psychiatry</u>. <u>www.youtube.com</u>

Lamy. L. (1981) New Light on Ancient Knowledge. Egyptian Mysteries. Thames & Hudson,
London, UK.

Maret. K (2014<u>) The Science of Melanin</u>. <u>www.youtube.com</u>

Melanin Research Foundation (2015<u>) Melanin: Energy from light and the soul's ascent</u>. Book
Shed Publishers.

Reiter. R.J. & Robinson. J (1996) <u>Melatonin.</u> Bantam Books, New York, USA.

Simon (2018) _Substantia nigra-The Science of Parkinson's._ https://scienceofparkinsons.com

Steiger. B. (1978) _Worlds Before Our Own._ Anomalist Books, San Antonio, Texas, USA.

Tellinger. M. (2013) _African Temples of the Anunnaki. The lost Technologies of the Gold Mines of Enki._ Bear & Company, Toronto, Canada.

Valentine. P. (2018) Matter Follows Mind. The truth about how your reality gets created. April 28th: https://www.youtube.com

Bonus Material

Olmec Civilization

Olmec Civilization

Printed in Great Britain
by Amazon

33686590R00016